The Getting Better Book

By Claire Rayner

Illustrated by Tony King

Piccolo Books

For Katy and Amy Stern
to help them be well

Contents

First published 1985 by
André Deutsch Ltd

This Piccolo edition published 1986 by Pan Books Ltd,
Cavaye Place, London SW10 9PG
Text copyright © 1985 by Claire Rayner
Illustrations © 1985 by Tony King
9 8 7 6 5 4 3 2 1
ISBN 0 330 29358 3
Printed in England by Chorley & Pickersgill Ltd, Leeds

Being Well

Your body is very clever.
Your brain thinks and your eyes see and your ears hear.
Your arms move, and legs kick and your fingers and toes wave and dance.
You breathe and you eat and you grow and you laugh and you cry.
You do all the things your body is made to do.
And most of the time you feel well.
Being well means being comfortable.
Your skin feels smooth and comfortable.

Your arms and legs feel strong and comfortable.
Your inside feels quiet and comfortable.
Everything about you feels just the way you like it to feel.
Most of the time you feel so comfortable you don't feel your body at all.
You don't think, "My skin feels smooth."
You don't think, "My arms and legs feel strong."
You don't think, "My inside feels quiet."
You just enjoy being you.

Being Ill

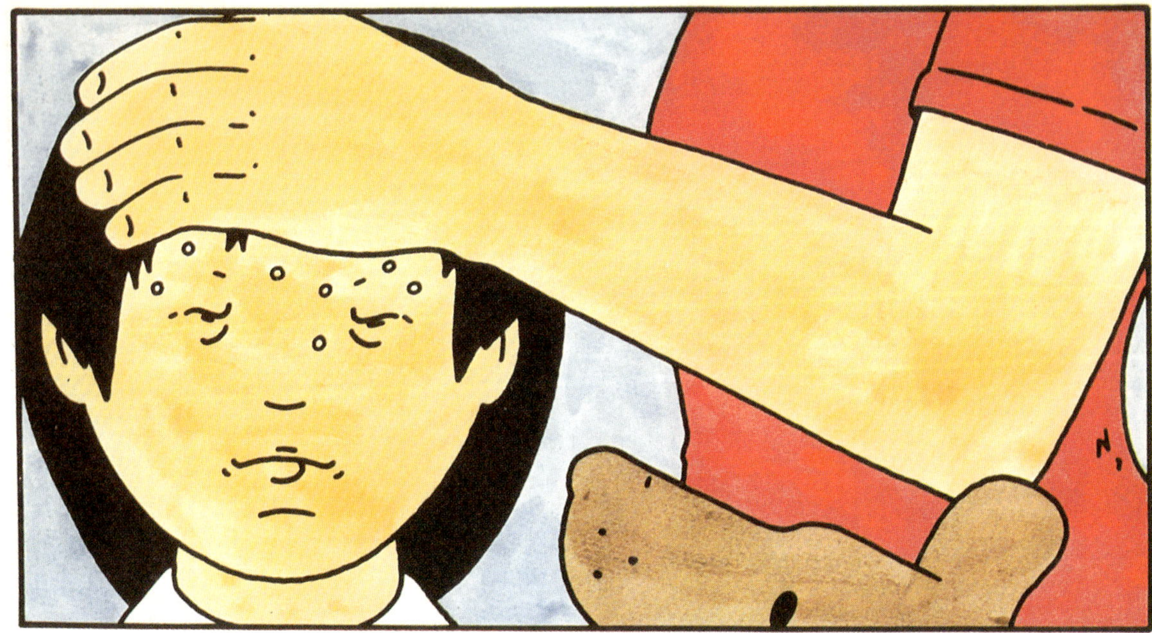

But people can't be well all the time.
Sometimes your body stops feeling the way you like it to feel.
Your skin feels hot and sweaty and itchy.
Your arms and legs feel tired and heavy and sore.
Your inside feels stirred up and sick and it aches.
And you think about how bad you feel all the time.

Why does that happen?

Sometimes it happens because of infections.
You can catch coughs and colds.
You can catch mumps and chicken pox and German measles.
You can catch sickness and belly aches.

Lots of people have lots of infections.

Sometimes it happens because of an accident.
Knives can cut you.
Roads can graze you when you fall down on them.
Hot things can burn you.
Hard and heavy things can break your bones.
Lots of people have lots of accidents.

Sometimes it happens because of sadness.
Being lonely can make your belly ache.
Being angry can make your head hurt.
Being frightened can make you sick.
Lots of people hurt because they are sad.

Sometimes it happens because a person's body isn't made as it should be.

Feet can be born shaped the wrong way so that they can't walk easily.

Eyes can be born looking the wrong way so that they can't see properly.

Insides can be born working the wrong way so that they can't do their job comfortably.

Brains can be born behaving the wrong way so they can't think so quickly.

Not many people are born with bodies that don't do their job properly. Happily most of those who are can be made well again by doctors.

Soon this book will tell you how.

But first, let's find out about germs and how they can make people ill.

Good Germs and Bad Germs

People aren't the only creatures who live in this world.
this world.
There are animals and birds and fishes too.
Some are very big.
Some are very small.

And some are so tiny you can't see them at all.

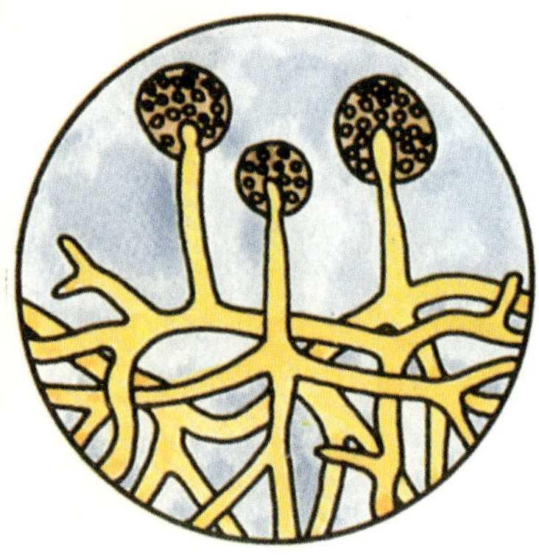

Funguses

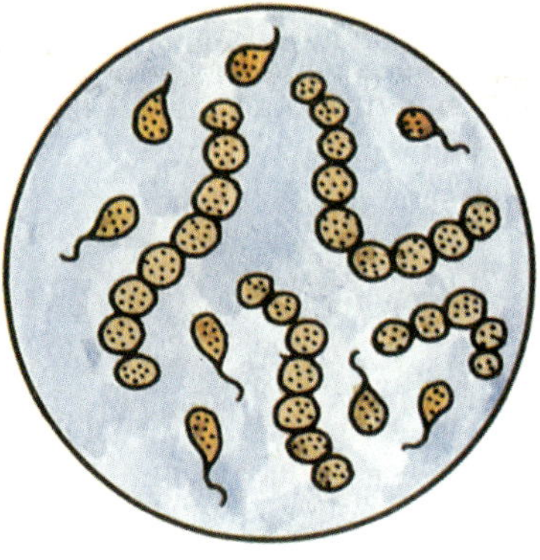

Bacteria

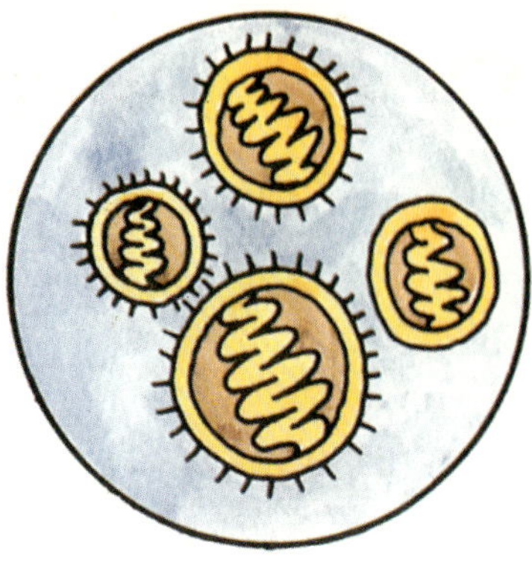

Viruses

Germs are like that.
There are some small ones called funguses.
There are some very small ones called bacteria.
There are some even smaller ones called viruses.
There are hundreds and hundreds and *hundreds* of different kinds of germs.
Some of them are very useful to us.
When they get into milk, they turn it into cheese or yoghurt, and that is very delicious for you.
When they get into grape juice they turn it into wine and that is very delicious for your parents.
Some of them are not at all useful to us.
When they get inside us, they give us colds and aches and pains and swellings and high temperatures and being sick and German measles and mumps and chicken pox.
How do they do that?

You can see funguses and bacteria through a microscope.

Sniffs and Splutters

One day you play with a friend who has a cold.
Your friend sneezes.
The germs which are making your friend's cold get thrown out into the air that you are breathing.
The cold germs, which are viruses, get into your nose when you breathe. Now you have been infected by the germs.

That night, while you are sleeping, the germs settle into your nose –
and your throat –
and your chest –
and start to have big families. Just a few germs can become millions after just a few hours.
They are very clever at growing.

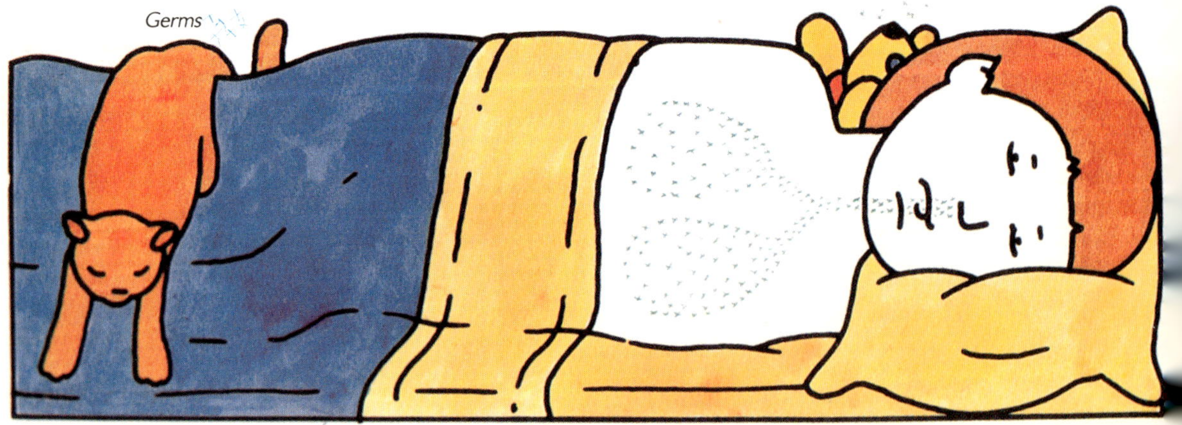

When there are a lot of germs they make the inside of your nose tickle.
They make your throat hot and dry and sore.
They make your chest tight and uncomfortable.
They make you feel ill and miserable.

But they can't do just what they like.
Inside your body there are special fighters, who don't like germs.
They are called antibodies.

As soon as they find out nasty germs have arrived in your body, they rush to the place where the germs are to fight them and get rid of them.

These special fighters are made by your body to fight off every kind of germ.
Each germ has its own special antibody to fight it.
But because your body doesn't know which germs are going to get into you, it can't make all the antibodies you need in advance.
So, every time a new germ gets into you, your body goes to work to make special antibodies for it.
Then the next time the same germ arrives in you, the special antibodies are there waiting. They won't let the germs get in and start to have big families.
They throw them out so fast you don't get ill.
That is why you can only get German measles once.
And you only get chicken pox once.
And you only get mumps once.
But you get lots of coughs and colds, because there are so many hundreds and hundreds and *hundreds* of different cold germs.

But cheer up! As you grow older and older
— and have more and more coughs and colds

– your body will develop more and more antibodies and you'll have fewer and fewer coughs and colds.
Have you ever noticed how many more colds you get than grown ups do?

Now you know why.

While the antibodies are being made to fight off the germs of your cold, there are other fighters in your body which can get rid of germs.
There are special bits in your blood called cells. Some of them, which are called white blood cells, can gobble up germs.
Like this

There are places in your body where there are armies of germ-gobblers.
These places are called glands.
They are in your neck –
and under your arms –
and in your groins –
and in lots of other parts of your body as well.
When germs get in your body the nearest gland to the place where they got in fills up with germ-gobbling cells.
They get swollen and a bit sore, because they are so full of busy cells.
But when all the germs have been gobbled up, or been fought by antibodies, the glands get small and comfortable again.

Your body does other things to get rid of germs.
Your brain tells your body to get hot, very hot, so hot that the germs are uncomfortable and can't do their job of making your nose tickle and your throat hot and sore and your chest tight.

When this happens you have a high temperature. You get red, and you sweat. The reason you sweat is to help you get cool. Being wet always feels cooler than being dry.
Isn't your body clever? It makes you hot to get rid of nasty germs, and makes you wet to help you be cool, all at the same time!

Your body also tries to wash the germs out.
It sends lots of extra water to your nose.
It is a special kind of water, rather sticky and sometimes rather thick. It catches the germs, and then runs out of your nose and takes the germs with it.
But it doesn't all run out. A lot stays inside your nose, catching the germs.
It makes your nose feel closed up.
You can't breathe through it any more.
You have to breathe through your mouth instead.
That makes your mouth feel nasty.
It makes your food taste different.
It makes your words sound funny.

You say,

instead of,

The same sticky water is sent to your chest. It catches the germs there too, and then it tickles your throat and makes you cough. Out comes the sticky water and out come the germs.

Sometimes the sticky water won't cough out easily. It sticks in your throat and stops your voice box from working properly. You get hoarse. When you talk it sounds as though you are growling like a dog.

Or purring like a kitten. Sometimes it hurts to talk, so people with colds are often quiet people. But sometimes people with colds are very noisy people. They make a very big sound indeed. That happens when the sticky water in their throats and in their noses tickles so much that the tickles turn into the biggest kind of cough there is. It's called a sneeze.

When it happens to you, you feel the tickle gets more and MORE

and MORE –

Until all of you feels like one big tickle and you just go –
A . . . TI . . . SHOOOOOOOOOOOOOOO-OOOOOO!
Millions of germs get thrown out when you do that.
Which is why it is important to put a handkerchief over your mouth and nose when you sneeze or when you cough.
Otherwise you give all your cold germs to someone else to make them have colds too.

But however careful you are, you can't stop all your germs getting to other people.
They are very clever at wriggling out of handkerchiefs and dancing about in the air, waiting to be breathed in by someone else.
But your body is much more clever than the germs. However many of them there are in you, and however much they make you cough – and sneeze –
and hurt your throat –
and stuff up your nose –
and make you feel ill and miserable –
your body wins the battle against them.
After feeling ill for a day or two, you begin to feel better.
You stop being so hot.
The thick water in your nose gets easier to blow out.
The thick water in your chest gets easier to cough out.
And soon the cold has gone away for ever.
But it has left behind its special antibodies to make sure you never get that cold again.
Although you may get a different one.
Isn't it a nuisance that there are so many different kinds of cold germs?

Who's Got Spots?

Sometimes people get germs that make
their throats sore –
and their noses blocked –
and their skin hot and sweaty –
and tickle them so that they cough and
sneeze –
but they haven't got ordinary colds at all.
They've caught German measles germs –
or chicken pox germs –
or mumps germs.
These are germs that like to settle down
and have big families in different parts of
your body, as well as your nose and throat.
German measles germs like to go to your
eyes and make them ache.
They like to go to your skin too. They make
spots there.

This is how people with German measles look.
Chicken pox germs also like to go to your skin, but they make a different sort of spot. *Itchy*
spots.

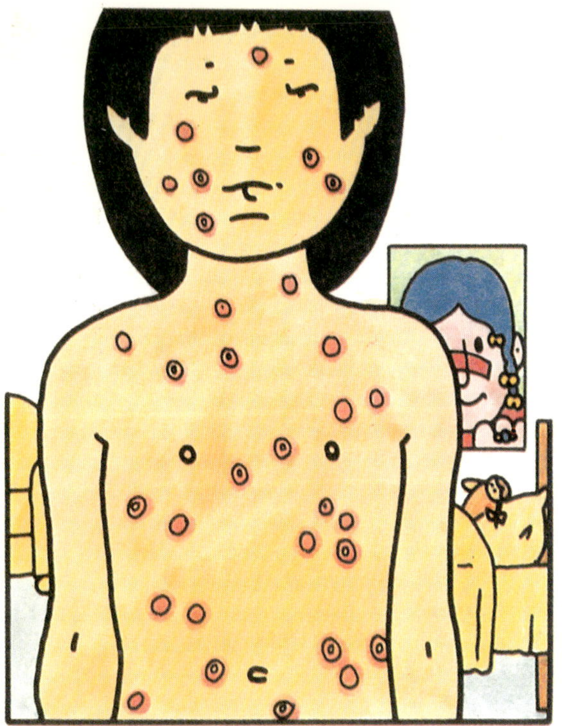

People with chicken pox look like this.
Mumps germs like to go to the place at the side of your face near your mouth where your spit is made. They make that place very lumpy and make your face hurt a lot.
Sometimes it happens on one side, when it looks like this –

And sometimes it happens on both sides, when it looks like this.

Mumps looks funny but it doesn't feel funny.

The best thing about German measles and chicken pox and mumps is that you can only get them once.
Can you remember why?

Upset Insides

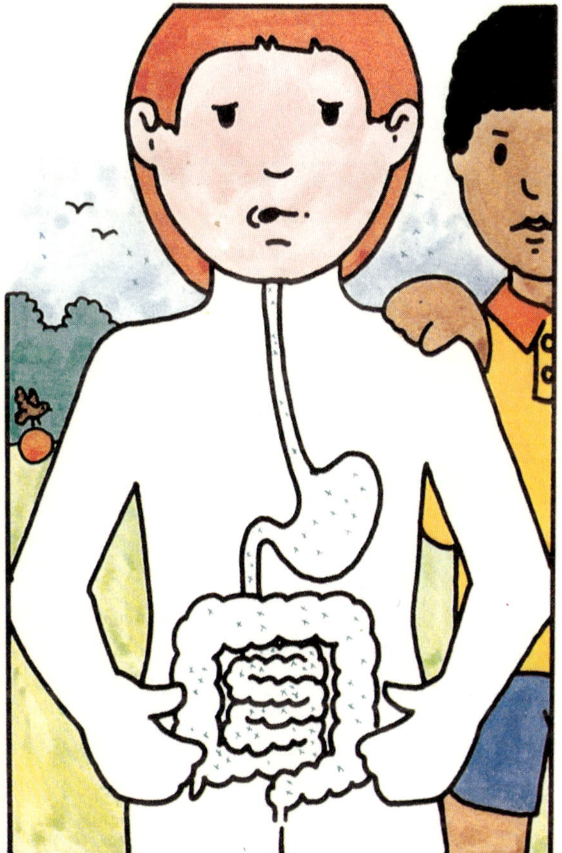

Not all the germs that get into you get in when you breathe.
Some of them get in when you eat and drink.
They go down inside you –
into your stomach –
and into your curled-up gut.
What happens when germs settle down and have big families in your stomach and your gut?
Your stomach doesn't like it at all.
Your gut doesn't like it at all.
They want to get rid of the germs as quickly as possible.
Your stomach does that by working backwards. Instead of pushing the food it collects out through its bottom door, into your gut –
It sends the food back through its top door –

And you are sick.
Feeling sick is one of the nastiest feelings there is.

Being sick is quite nasty, too.
But afterwards you feel so much better that
you don't mind so much.

It's not only germs that make people sick.
Eating too much food too quickly can make
you sick.
Your stomach doesn't like getting a sudden
load of food in through the top door and
sends it smartly back.

Eating lots of different mixed up foods can
make you sick.
Your stomach doesn't like mixtures like
pickled gherkins and fizzy lemonade and
sour green apples and sweet ice-cream and
potatoes and puddings and pies and herrings
and ham and honey and hot dogs and
hamburgers.
They are very good on their own, but
altogether they make stomachs very sick.

What happens when germs get into your
gut?

Your gut wants to get rid of them, just as
your stomach does.
It's too far to send your waste food back up
through your stomach.
So, it hurries it along its long, long tube —
so fast that the water in your waste food
doesn't get a chance to go into your blood.
When the food gets to the end of the tube,
it's very watery.
It is so watery, and in so much of a hurry to
get out that you have to keep rushing to
the lavatory to let it get out.
It gets out of the little hole in your bottom
which is the end of the tube.
When the waste food is in a hurry to get
out, it is called diarrhoea.
Some people call it squitters, because that is
the sort of sound the watery waste makes
when it comes out of the little hole at the
end of your gut in a hurry.
Whatever you call it, sometimes it hurts.
You have a bellyache.
You have it because your stomach and gut
are having to work extra hard to get rid of
the germs.
People who have sickness and diarrhoea
and bellyache sometimes feel tired and
miserable. This is because of the germs and

16

also because they are losing a lot of useful water when they get rid of the germs.
Your body needs water to be comfortable; without enough water a body would be like a dried up old prune –
or a raisin.
Drinking lots of water, slowly, in sips, helps

people who have sickness and diarrhoea to feel a bit better.
They don't need to eat much food, but they do need to drink lots of water.
When they do, their bodies find it easier to make antibodies and get rid of the germs that are making the sickness and diarrhoea happen.

Inside Upsets

It is not only germs that make people feel sick.
It is not only eating too much food too quickly that makes people feel sick.
Sometimes people are sick because they are unhappy about something.
Sometimes people get bellyaches because they are unhappy about something.
Sometimes people get headaches because they are unhappy about something.
Perhaps they are frightened.
Perhaps they are lonely.
Perhaps they are angry.
Suppose your mother is cross one day? That can make you feel frightened.
Suppose there is no one at school you like to play with? That can make you feel lonely.
Suppose your father has gone away and not told you why or where?
That can make you feel angry.
Feelings like this start inside your head, where you think but they can spread and spread —
and go into your stomach and your gut.
So when your mother is cross you get a headache.
When you have to go to school you get sick.
When your father goes away you get diarrhoea.
Sometimes you can make your headache

and bellyache and sickness better if you tell
people how you feel.
Say, "I am frightened when you get cross."
Say, "I have no one to play with at school."

Say, "I don't want daddy to go away."
See if that makes the bad feelings go away.
It might.

Eyes and Ears and Noses

Is there anywhere else in you that germs can go and make you ill?
Yes there is.
They can get in your eyes
and in your ears
as well as in your nose.

If germs get in your eyes they can sometimes make them very red and sore. They make tears come out all the time, even when you aren't crying. Some of the tears go down inside your face to your nose when you have germs which make your eyes pink.
Then you sniff a lot.
Your eyes go red and make lots of tears to wash out the germs that have got in.
It's important not to rub pink eyes because that stops the work of washing out the germs.
You mustn't rub even though your eyes itch a lot because of the germs stamping about in them.
It's hard to stop yourself rubbing, but you

have to try. If you rub them you make the germs spread about even more.
You mustn't rub your eyes on towels, in case someone else comes and rubs their eyes too.
Then they will catch the germs that will make their eyes pink, too.
When you have pink eyes, your doctor will give you special medicine for them.
The medicine gets rid of the germs.

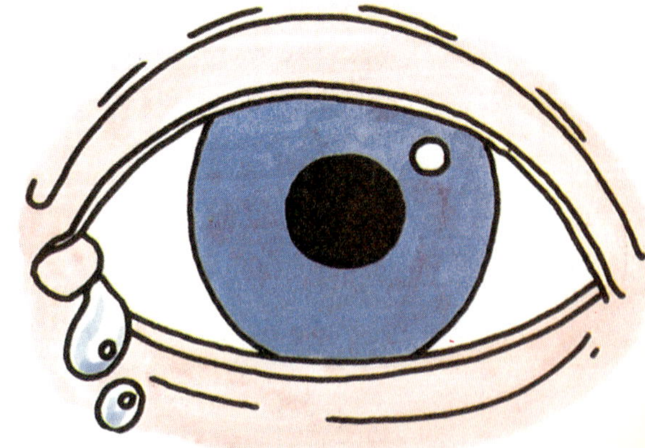

The medicine is put right inside your eye where the germs are. It is put in in tiny drops, or in a strip of ointment.
It tickles when it goes in, but it's worth the tickle. It gets rid of the germs.
This is the best way to have drops or ointment put in your eyes.

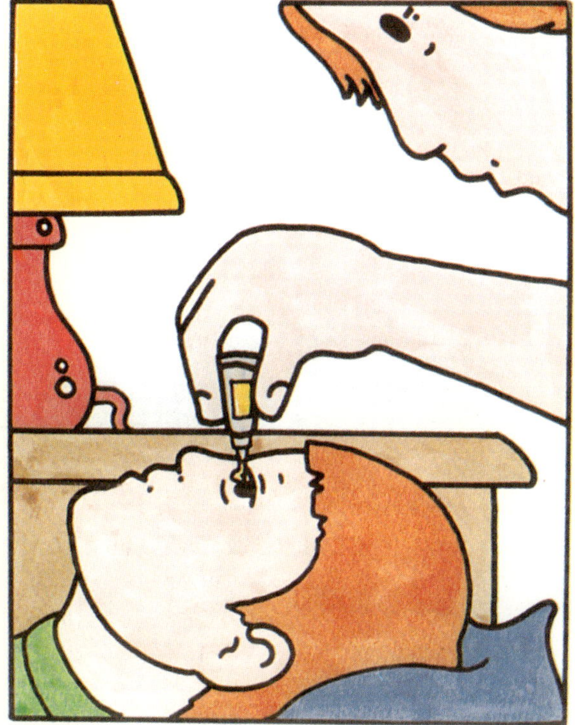

Sometimes ointment is put in eyes to get rid of little spots that come on the edges of eyelids.
The spots happen because a few germs squeeze in through the tiny space where one of your eyelashes is joined on.
The spots are called styes.
It is a good name for them, because when you have a stye, it feels so big you think you've got a pig in your eye.
But you haven't. If the special drops or ointment are put in, the spot soon goes away, and there is no pig left there at all!

It isn't only germs that spoil the way eyes work.

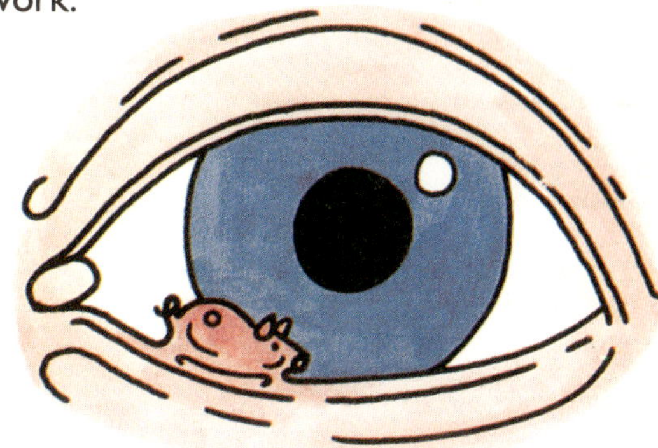

Sometimes people are born with eyes that don't work properly.
When people are born with eyes that look the wrong way, they have a squint.
Squints can be changed, so that both eyes look in the same direction at once as they are supposed to do.
They can be changed by wearing special glasses.

They can be changed by having an operation.
It takes quite a long time to make squinting eyes straight, but it's important to do it, because straight eyes work better than squinting ones.

Sometimes eyes look straight but can't see properly.
Some things look fuzzy, like this.

Some things look small, like this.

Wearing glasses makes the fuzzy things look clear —
And the small things look the right size.
The world is full of people who wear glasses all the time to help their eyes see properly.
Isn't it a good thing glasses were invented to help eyes?

Sometimes germs get into ears.
They can get in from outside —
or they can creep in through the back way, climbing up a tube that is between your nose and your ears. Sometimes people who have colds in their noses get pains in their ears because germs have crept up into them through the back way.
Earaches are especially nasty. They hurt a lot. They make you feel sick.
Sometimes they make you be sick.
Usually they make you have a high temperature. And then you sweat and ache and feel sad and sorry.
When people have earaches, doctors give

them medicine to get rid of the germs that are making the ache.

Sometimes the medicine is put in through the ear, in drops.

This is the best way to have the drops put in.

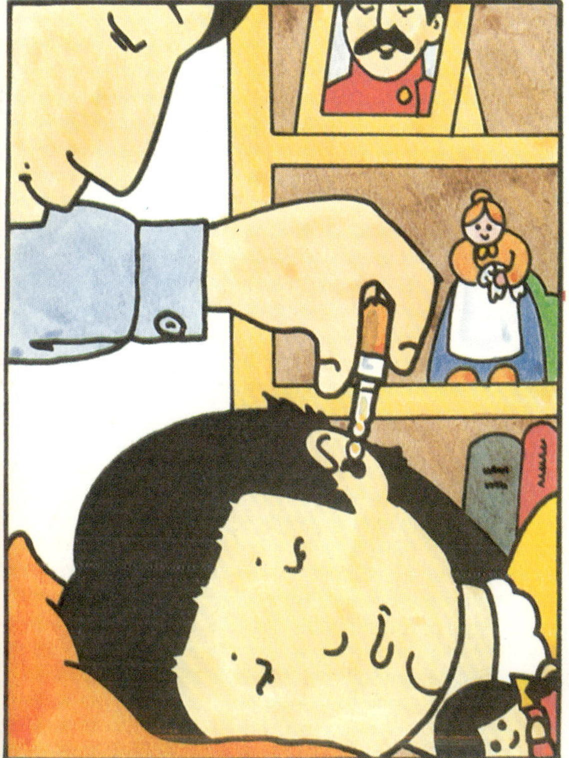

Ask the person putting the drops in to make them a little warm, first.

Cold drops going into your ear are uncomfortable, and make you ache more.

Warm drops going in are kind, and make you feel better.

Sometimes the medicine is put inside your whole body, to kill all the germs everywhere.

In your nose –

In your ears –

In your stomach –

Everywhere.

The medicine goes all over your body in your blood, and when it gets to your ears it gets rid of the germs there and gets rid of the ache.

When people have germs in their ears they can't always hear properly.

When people talk to them everything sounds muffled.

Then when the germs are gone, everything sounds LOUD again.

But sometimes, when the germs have gone, they leave behind some of the sticky water inside the ear.

Then everything goes on sounding muffled even though the pain has gone away.

This is called a glue ear, because the thick water is as sticky as glue.

The doctor has to put special little tubes into the ear to let all the sticky glue get out.

The tubes are called grommets

They have to stay in ears quite a long time to do their work.

Then they can be taken out (or they fall out by themselves).

If you have to have grommets in your ears, sometimes you can't go swimming, in case

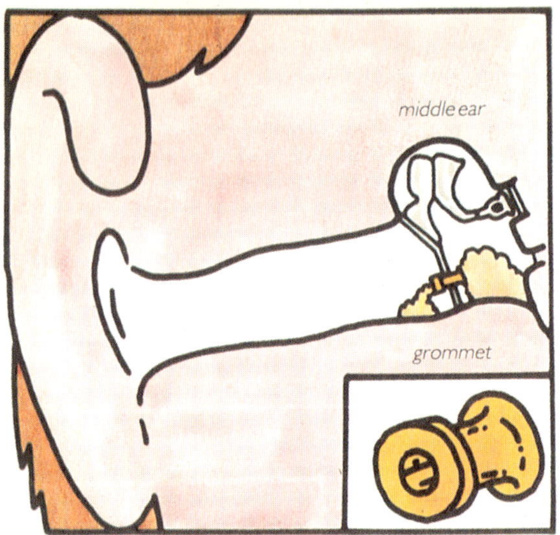

You may need medicine to get rid of the germs.
You don't need medicine for an ordinary cold. Only if your sinuses get blocked up. If you do need medicine, it may be the same one that doctors give people with sore throats —
or pink eyes —
or ear aches.
It is medicine called an antibiotic, because it fights germs.
Penicillin is an antibiotic medicine.

the swimming water gets right inside your ear.
It's a nuisance if you can't go swimming for a while, but not so much of a nuisance as hearing everything muffled.

When germs get into noses they may make them blocked up —
or they make the spaces inside your head near your nose, which are called sinuses, blocked up —
and that can make your face ache a lot.

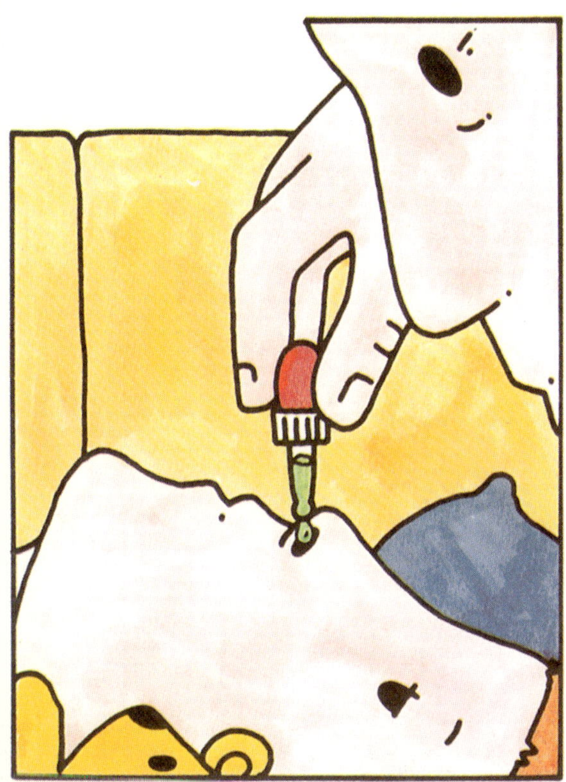

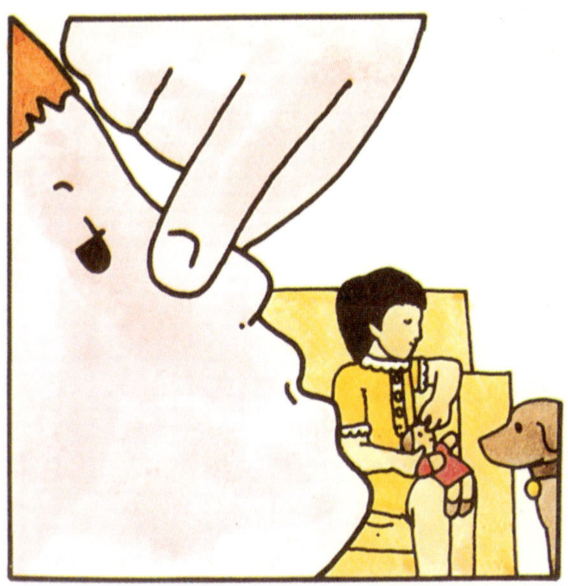

Sometimes the medicine for noses is put in
in drops.
Having nose drops put in feels funny. The
drops drip down the back of your throat
inside and make you swallow and cough.
But the drops help to get germs out of
noses.

Sometimes noses start to bleed inside.
This can make a big mess.
Some people have funny ideas about how to
stop noses from bleeding.
They put cold keys down the person's back—
Or lumps of ice — brrrr!
But the best way to stop a nose from
bleeding is to pinch it yourself, like this.
Then the bleeding will stop.

Scratches and Wallops and Bumps

Why do parts of your body bleed?
Blood is very important.
It is full of food –
and water –
and antibodies –
(do you remember all about antibodies?)

and even some of the air you breathe in.
It travels all over your body taking the food
and the water and the bits of air and the
antibodies to all the places in your body
where they are needed.
When your smallest toe needs food and
water to make it do its work of wiggling,
your blood carries it there.
When your big round bottom needs food
and water to help it do its job of sitting,
your blood takes it there.
Blood travels round you in special tubes
called veins and arteries.

Some of them are very BIG

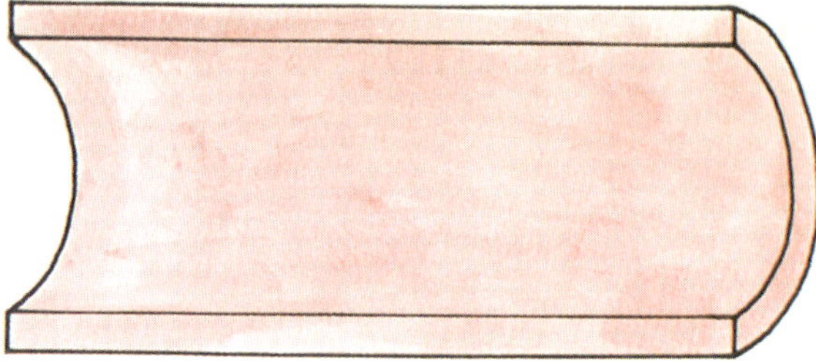

And some are tiny –

And they are all over your body.
Everywhere.

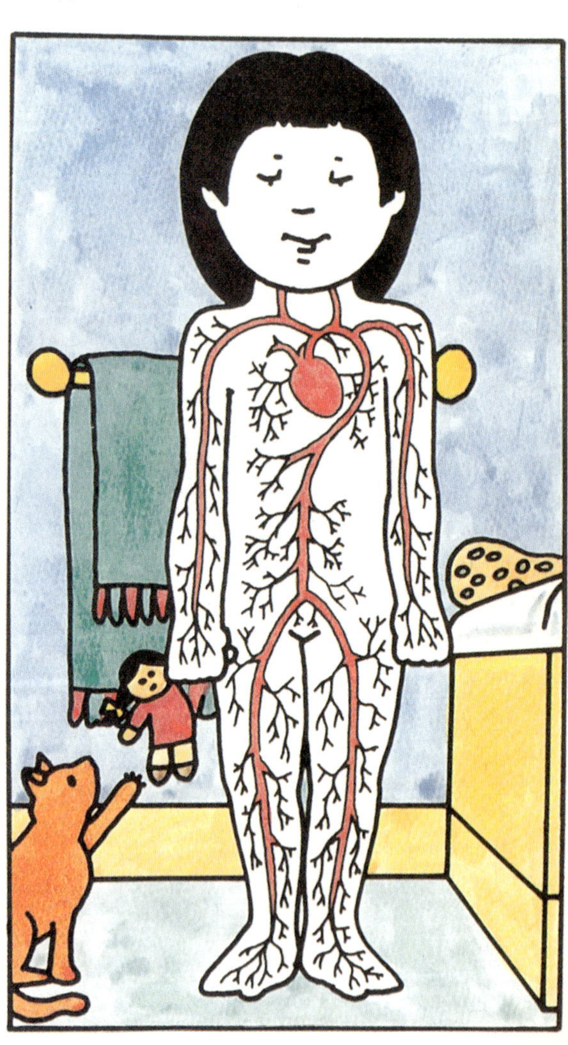

Usually your skin keeps all the blood tubes safely inside you.
But sometimes your skin gets a little broken.
Perhaps you rub your skin on a rose thorn.
That is called a scratch.
Perhaps you fall on the road and scrape your skin.
That is called a graze.
Sometimes you handle a knife or a sharp piece of glass or a rough tin in the wrong way and tear your skin.
That is called a cut.
When that happens the tubes of blood inside your skin get broken too.

And out comes the blood, all thick and warm and sticky.
This is a pity because it wastes the useful blood.
It also makes your clothes messy.
And it hurts.
But your body is clever.
As soon as the blood comes out of your body and meets the air, some special little bits in your blood, which are called platelet cells —
huddle up together. It's as though they don't like the cool air.
They huddle closer and closer together —
Till they stick together in a thick lump.
This is called a clot.

And do you know what the clot does?
It plugs up the broken bit of skin.
It plugs up the broken tubes.
Now the blood can't get out any more!
And the germs can't get in.
The clot sits on top of the scratch or the graze or the cut and stops it hurting too much.
It gets thicker and thicker and harder and harder.
Now it is called a scab.
A scab is useful, because underneath it the tubes join up again —

the torn skin begins to join up again —
and get smooth and stretchy again —
and one day the scab falls off, and there you
are, with mended tubes and new skin!
But there is a special problem with
scratches and grazes and cuts.
Can you imgine what it is?
When your skin is broken, something could
get into your body through the break,
couldn't it?
What could that something be?
Yes! You guessed right.
Germs.
What happens when germs get in through
scratches and grazes and cuts?
Your body sends some more special germ
fighters to get rid of them.
Not just antibodies this time, but *white*
blood cells.
These rush to where the germs are and
swallow them up. Whole!
They are the same sort of cells that live in
the glands, which get big and sore when
germs get into your body through your
nose, or your mouth, or your ears.
But they don't only live in the glands. They
can travel around your body in your blood.
When germs get into you through a scratch
or a graze or a cut, so many of them come
to it that the place where the cut or graze
is gets hot and sore and swollen.
The dead germs turn into thick yellowish
greenish stuff.

This is called pus.
When all the germs are killed and made into
pus, it comes out of the cut or the graze —
And then the skin can grow again and mend
you.
If you are quick when you have an accident
you can stop germs getting in and having to
be killed by white cells, so that the place
gets hot and sore and full of pus.
You can put on special germ-killing
medicine.
Some germ-killing medicines hurt your cut
or graze when you put them on, but it's
better to have a little hurt like that, than
the bigger hurt of a hot swollen pus-filled

The glands

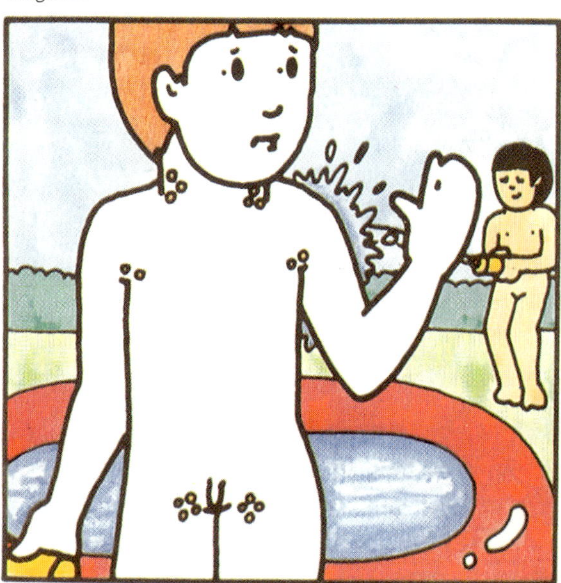

place on your skin, isn't it?
So let people put medicine on cuts and
grazes.
And sticky plaster or bandages to keep the
place clean and keep germs out.
It's the best way to help your skin be
mended quickly.
Sometimes, a cut on the skin is so big that it
needs help to grow again.
It looks like this —

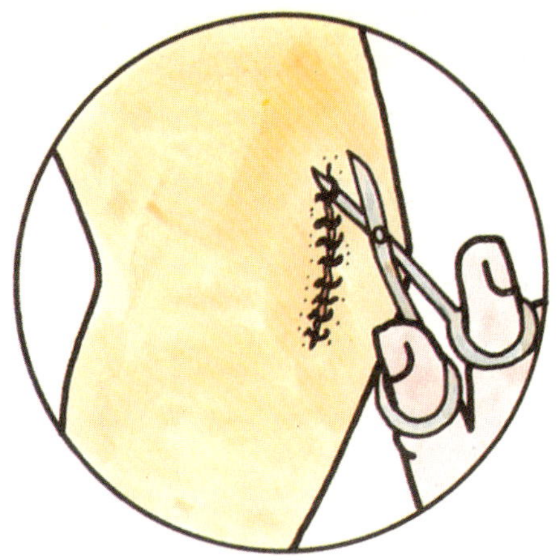

Like this.
As long as you keep very still when they are
being taken out, they shouldn't be too
uncomfortable.
But sometimes it does hurt a little.
But it's worth the hurt, because they help
make your cut skin whole again.

When skin grows together again after a cut
or graze, it sometimes grows thicker and
stronger than it used to be.
It looks a different colour.
Sometimes darker than the other skin.
Sometimes lighter than the other skin.
This is called a scar.

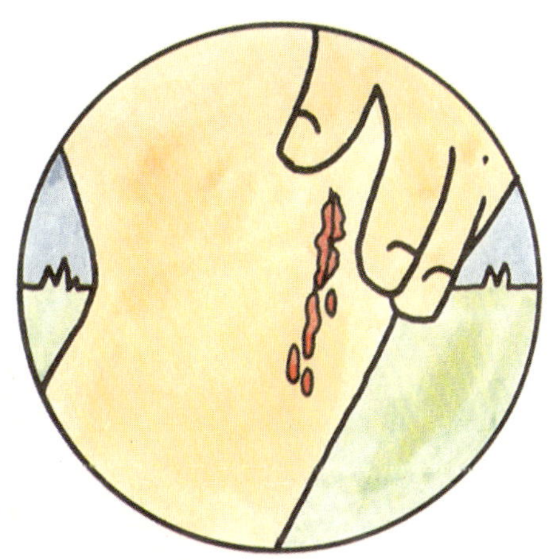

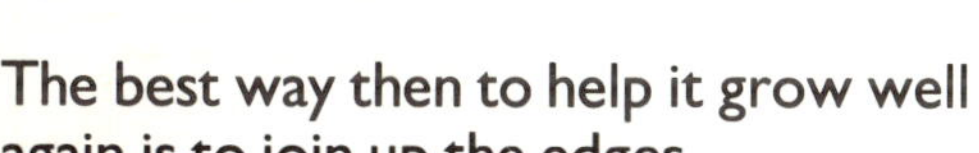

The best way then to help it grow well
again is to join up the edges.
That can be done in just the same way as
the edges on a tear in your shirt are joined
up.
With stitches!
Having stitches put in a cut feels
uncomfortable, but when doctors do their
sewing, they put special pain-stopping
medicine there first.
This is called an anaesthetic.
That is a Greek word which means "no
feeling".
After a few days, when the skin edges have
grown together, the stitches aren't needed
any more.
They have to be taken out.

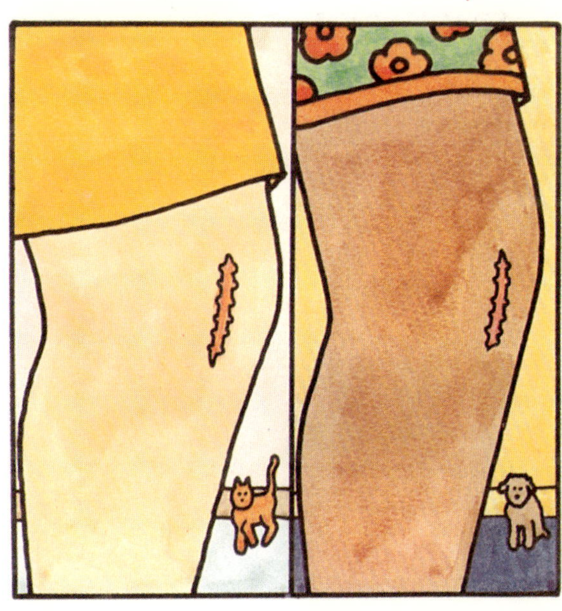

Sometimes they last for ever.
Ask your grown ups if they have any scars from cuts they had when they were your age.
They probably have. Most of the people in the world have scars.

Sometimes a strange thing happens when a person has an accident.
Blood gets out of its tiny tubes, because the tubes get a hard wallop.
But the skin isn't torn or scraped, so the blood can't get out of your body.
Instead, it pushes against your skin inside —
and pushes and pushes —
and you get a great big bump.
Sometimes you don't get a bump, because there is plenty of room under your skin at that place for the blood to be.
But it feels sore and it hurts.
This is called a bruise.
If you have a pale skin, you can see a bruise.
It looks bluish red.
Or reddish blue.
Because blood isn't just bright red. There's quite a lot of blue in it.
Like this.

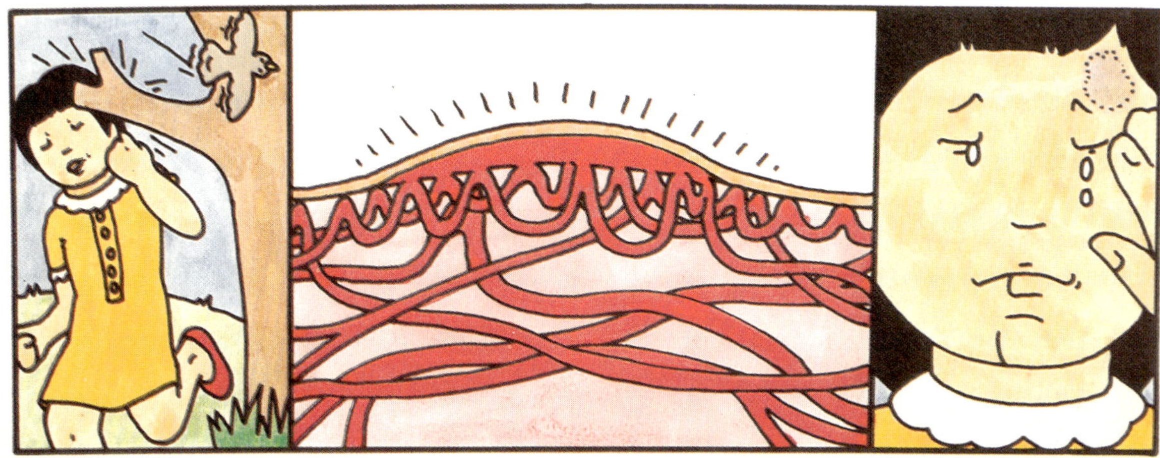

When you have a bruise, your body starts to be clever again.
It sends more special cells to the place to mop up the blood that was spilled out of the tubes.
The mopping up takes a few days, and while it happens your bruise changes colour.
It gets lighter —
and lighter —
and stops being reddish blue
or bluish red —
and starts being yellow!

There are more colours in your blood than you knew, aren't there?
Just as there is food, and air and water and all sorts of other useful things your body needs.

Accidents and very hard wallops can do more than break your skin and make the blood come out of its little tubes.
If the wallop is hard enough it can break the hardest part of you.
A bone.

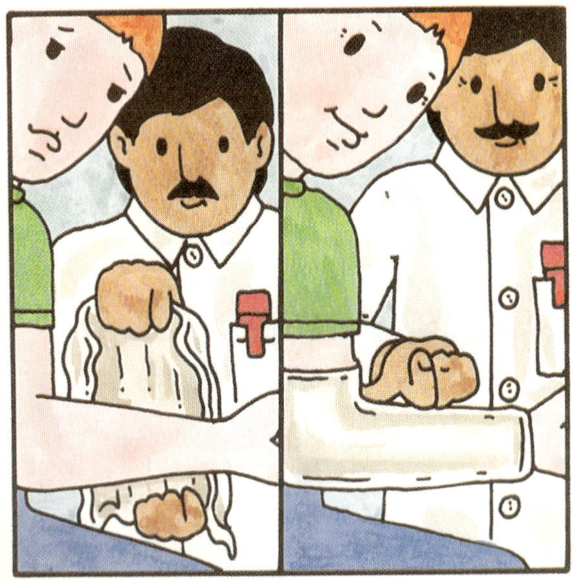

Broken bones hurt a lot.
They take a long time to grow together again.
They need a doctor's help to grow together again straight and strong.
The doctor has to put on a special kind of bandage to keep the edges of the broken bone neatly together so that they can grow together straight and strong.
This bandage is called a plaster.
When it is put on it is wet and floppy.
But after a while it gets drier,
and drier,
and drier –
and almost as hard as bone!
People with plasters on can still walk about, as long as they are careful.
They can enjoy themselves asking their friends to draw pictures on them.
To find out if the bone has grown together safely under the plaster, the doctor takes a special kind of photograph of you.
It is called an X-ray.
It looks inside your skin and your muscles and your blood to your bones.
When the X-ray photograph shows the bone has joined up properly, the doctor takes the plaster off.
It doesn't hurt to have plaster taken off, but

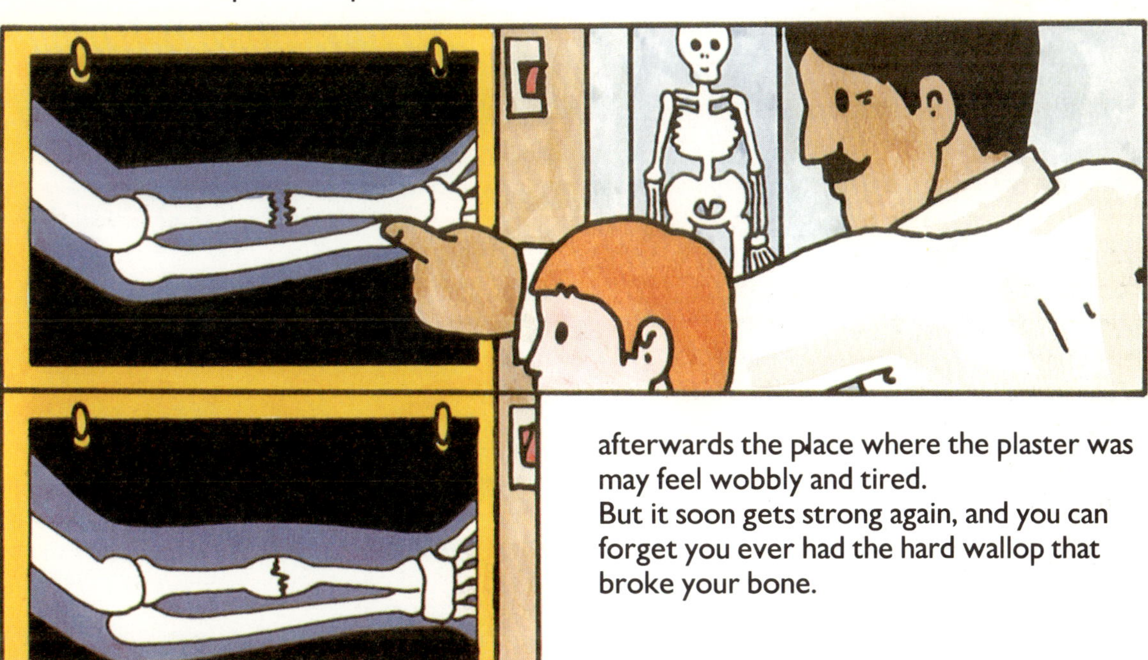

afterwards the place where the plaster was may feel wobbly and tired.
But it soon gets strong again, and you can forget you ever had the hard wallop that broke your bone.

Hot Can Hurt

It isn't only wallops that can hurt you.
So can hot things.
Fires and kettles and hot taps and tea pots can hurt you a lot.
Electricity can hurt you a lot.
People must always be careful with hot things and electrical things.
If your skin is touched by something hot, your body tries to make a cushion over the burned part to keep it safe from hurting. The cushion is full of water. It is called a blister.
Sometimes people want to break a blister to let all the water out, but that is silly.
A flat cushion doesn't protect anything!
If you leave a blister alone, the burned skin it is protecting slowly grows smooth and comfortable again –
and then the blister shrivels up and disappears by itself and you can peel off the left-over bits of it.

When you sit or play in the hot sun too long lots of your skin can get burned.
It doesn't make big blisters but it may peel off to show new skin underneath.
It can hurt while it is peeling.

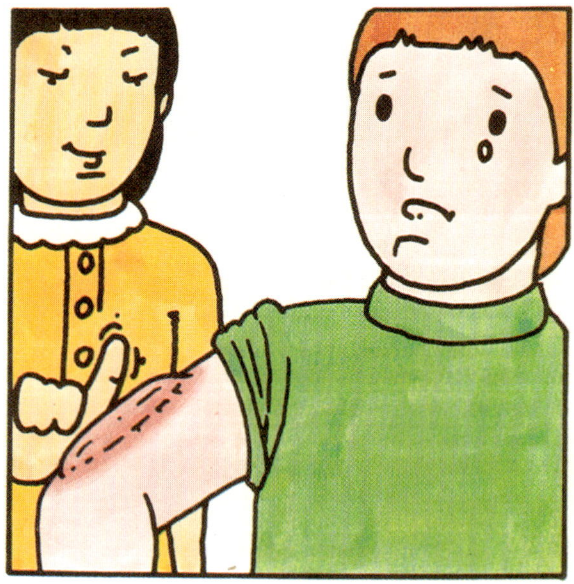

Sitting or playing in the hot sun for too long is not good for your skin. It is better to wear a shirt and a hat; if you don't want to wear them, then stay in the shade.

If you play in the sun for just a little time every day, your skin gets tanned, without hurting.

This is the body's clever way of making the skin stronger, so that the sun can't burn it.

It isn't only hot things that can hurt you and make blisters. Rubbing a piece of skin too much can make it so sore and so hot that the skin needs a cushion to protect the place.

This is why new shoes sometimes make blisters.

So, if you are taken to buy new shoes and they hurt when you try them on —
SAY SO! Even if they are very beautiful shoes.

If you don't, and they are bought for you, you may get blisters.

Itches and Pimples, Allergies and Invaders

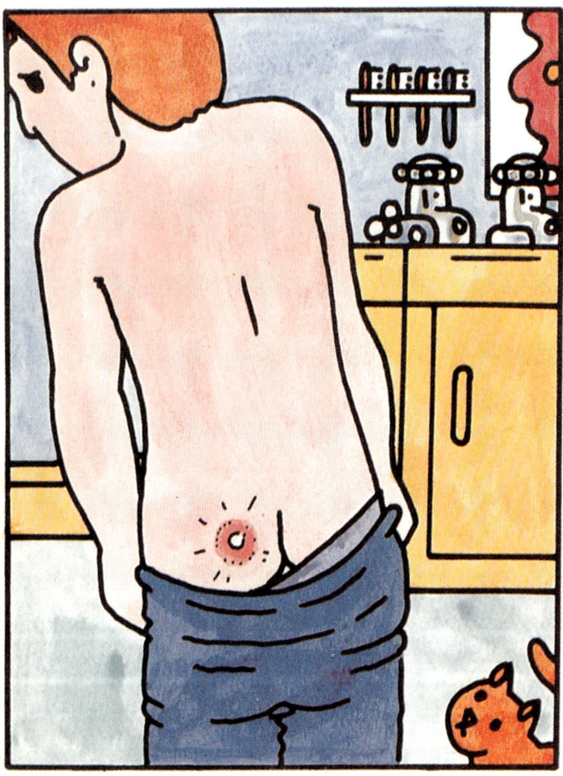

Sometimes your skin hurts even when you haven't scratched it or grazed it or cut it.
Sometimes a few germs get in through tiny spaces in your skin.
They are so tiny you can't see them, but the germs can, because they are tiny too.

They try to settle down and have big families, but the white cells come to stop them.
Then the place gets hot and sore and swollen and filled with pus, just as though you had a big cut where germs could get in.
If the hot sore place is a small one, then you have a pimple.
If it is a big one, then you have a boil.
Sometimes you need a bandage with special ointment on it to make the sore place better.
Pimples and boils always get better, because your white cells fight off the germs.
Having white cells is very useful for you.

Isn't your body clever to be able to fight the things that hurt you?
But though your body is clever, sometimes it makes mistakes.
It doesn't only fight germs which could hurt you.
It also fights things which can't hurt you.
Like pollen from grass and flowers.
Or sticky plasters which are put on cuts.
Or dust in the air, or cat hairs or dog hairs or birds' feathers or even things you like to eat, such as strawberries and milk.

When these things come near some
people's bodies, they get spots on their
skins, like this —

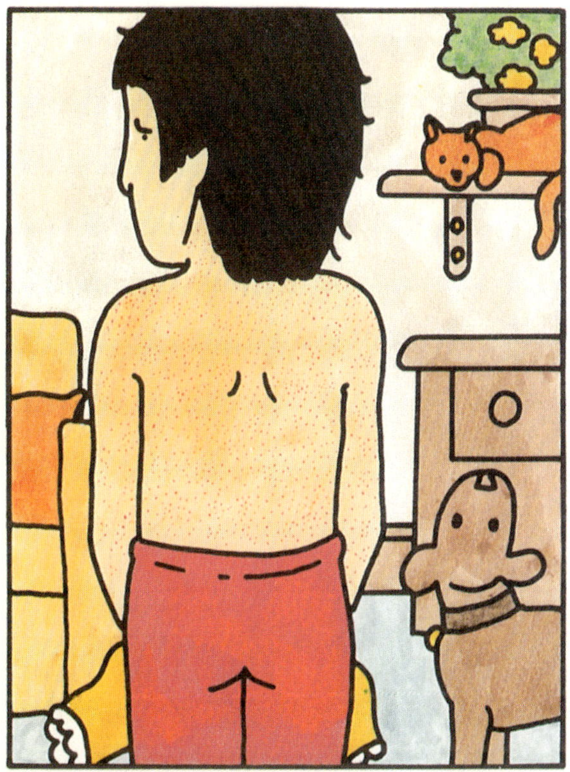

or they get sick —
or they get breathless and wheezy —
or their eyes get watery —
and their noses fill with extra sticky water —
and they feel very miserable indeed.
This is called having an allergy.
It happens because your body thinks that
pollen and plasters, cat hairs and dog hairs,
strawberries and milk, are the same as
germs.
Which is silly, because they aren't.
Sometimes the best way to stop the
problem is just to keep away from what
starts it.
Don't play in fields and gardens when there
is a lot of pollen about.
Don't play with cats and dogs.
Don't eat strawberries or milky foods and
drinks.

But sometimes that can't be done. People
can't hide away from *all* the things they are
allergic to. They can't always be sure what
they are.
So their bodies have to learn how to be
more sensible about what they fight.
Sometimes a doctor can give special
medicines which teach the body to stop
fighting things it need not fight.
A tiny bit of whatever-it-is that the body
fights by mistake is slipped in quietly with
a syringe.
This is called an injection.
Injections feel like being pricked with a
needle.
They aren't much fun, but they aren't all
that bad!
When the first tiny injection is given to a
person with an allergy, the body sends only
a few of its fighters to get rid of it, and
makes a little bit of an antibody.
There are so few fighters that there are no
rashes, and no itching and no wheezing.
Then, after a week or so, the doctor gives a
bit more of whatever-it-is the body fights,
and a bit more antibody is made —
And then, week after week, bigger and
bigger bits are given —
until at last the body has made lots of
antibodies and stops making such a silly fuss
about pollen and plasters, cat hairs and dog
hairs, strawberries and milk.
And the allergy problem doesn't happen
any more.
Not every person with an allergy needs lots
of injections.
Sometimes a doctor can give special
medicine to make the spots and the
sickness, the wheeziness and the wateriness
stop happening.
Sometimes the medicine is swallowed —
and sometimes it is breathed in —
whatever way it is given it helps the person
with an allergy feel much better.
It isn't only germs and allergies which can

make people get rashes and feel ill.
Sometimes insects like bees and wasps get
annoyed and sting a person.
Sometimes unfriendly plants like nettles
sting a person.
At once the body behaves as though germs
or allergies were at work, and sends
fighters to the place.
And once again there is a hot swollen sore
place, or a rash.
But they get better quickly, as long as you
don't scratch and rub them too much!

It isn't only germs and bees and wasps that
can get on to people's bodies.
Sometimes other creatures get on you and
make you itch and scratch.
Lots of people catch headlice.
These are tiny little insects, just big enough
to see, which like to live in warm clean hair.
They lay their eggs, which are called nits,
and stick them to your hairs, and then the
eggs hatch into more headlice.
And then you scratch and scratch and
scratch —
People who catch headlice are not bad or
dirty people.
They are just unlucky people, and usually
they are careful clean people. Nits like clean

hair best of all.
Happily it is not hard to get rid of headlice.
Your hair has to be washed with a special
shampoo —

And combed with a special comb —
and then the headlice have gone away.
Until perhaps you catch them again from
someone else!
But that won't happen if your mother
always uses the special comb to find if any
nits have arrived.
Something else that gets into people's
bodies are tiny little wriggling
threadworms.
They are like nits. They like nice clean
healthy people to live in best of all!
They get in when a person swallows one of
the tiny eggs that hatch into threads.

36

You might pick up the eggs by touching someone who has them and doesn't know it.
Or from the ground when you play on it — or from ordinary dust.
From almost anywhere.
When the eggs get inside your gut they hatch into the little wriggling threads.
Then when you go to the lavatory, they come out with your waste food.
They can be very troublesome. They make your bottom itch and itch and keep you awake at night.

But don't worry — threads are easy to lose! Special medicines can be swallowed which soon send the threads rushing out of your body for good and all.
And to make sure you don't get them again —

ALWAYS wash your hands after going to the lavatory.

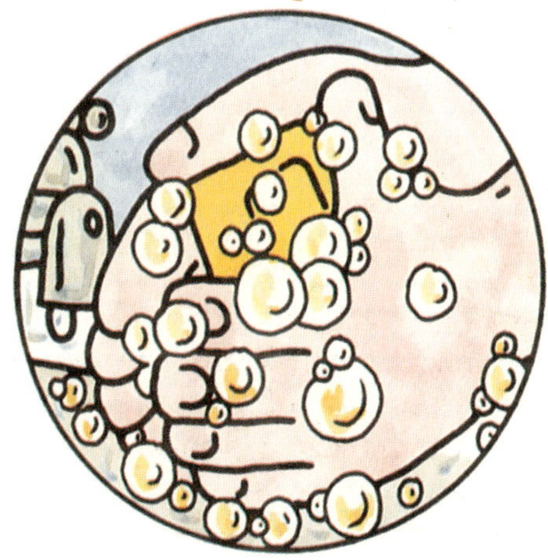

ALWAYS wash your hands before eating. Then you're less likely to swallow eggs again.
But if you do, don't worry. The medicine will soon get rid of them.

Operating Theatre
General Ward
Intensive Care Unit
Intensive Care Unit
General Ward
Kitchen
X-ray Dept.
Doctor's surgery
Waiting Room

Doctors and Nurses and Hospitals

Doctors and nurses work in different places.
Sometimes they work in their own houses. These are called surgeries.
Sometimes they work in schools.
Sometimes they visit ill people in their own houses.
Sometimes they work in hospitals.
Some people are frightened of hospitals, but that is silly.
Hospitals are interesting places, where everyone tries to help ill people get better.
Look at all the things that happen in hospital.

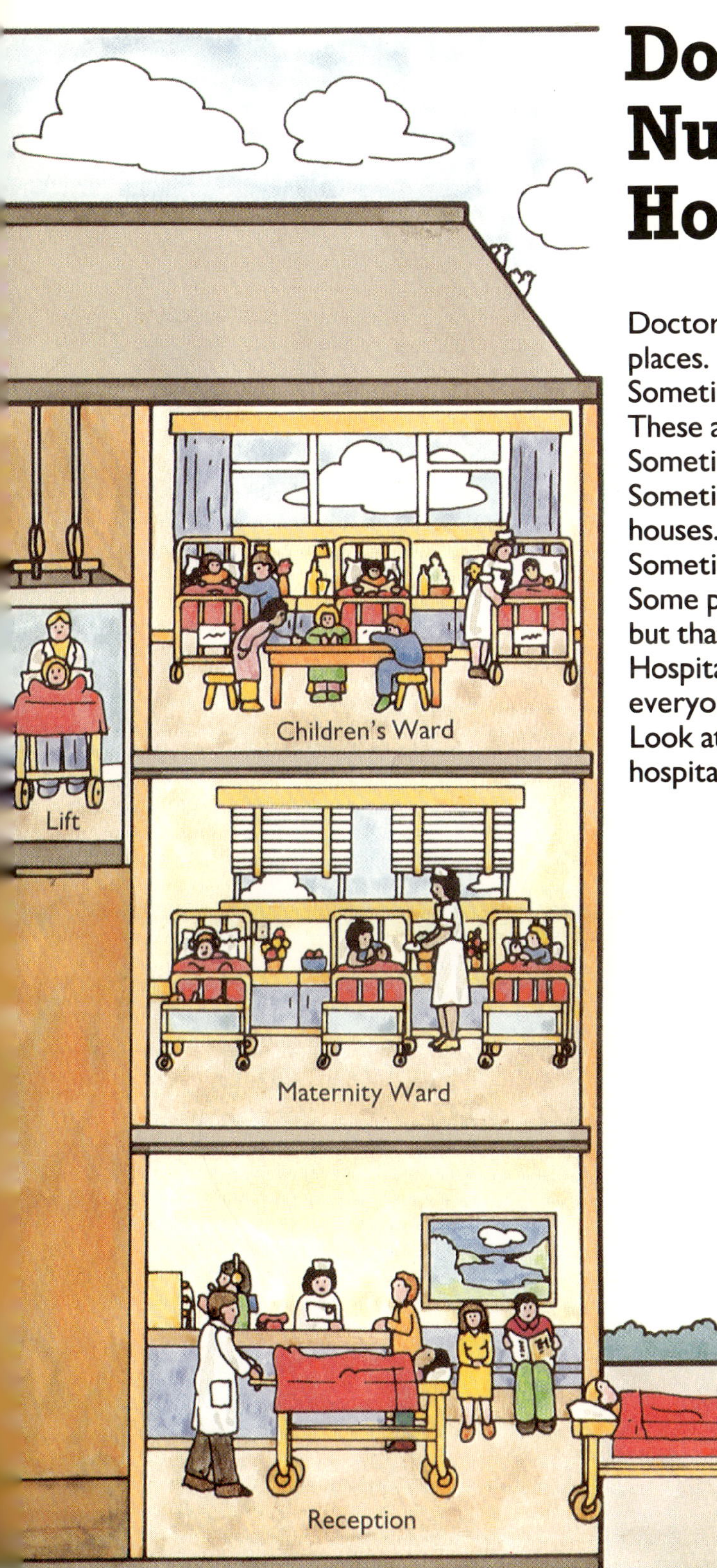

Can you see that the doctors and nurses are talking to the ill people?
They are explaining to them what is wrong with them, and how they can get well.
Just as this book does.
If you have to go to a hospital, remember to ask the doctors and nurses what they are doing and why they are doing it.

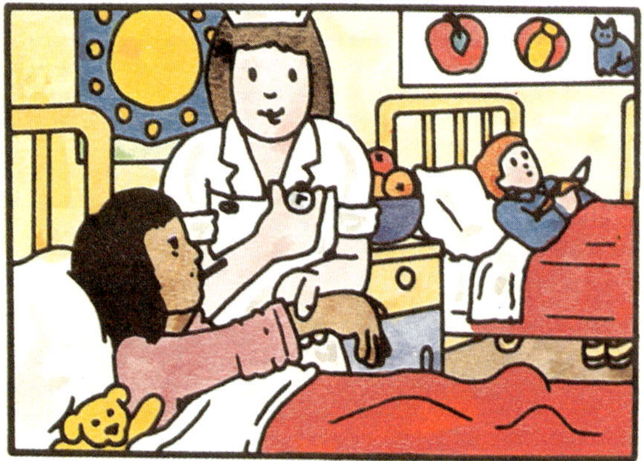

Ask the nurses why they sometimes put masks over their mouths and noses. Can you guess what they will say? Yes. It is to stop germs getting out of their mouths and noses into you.

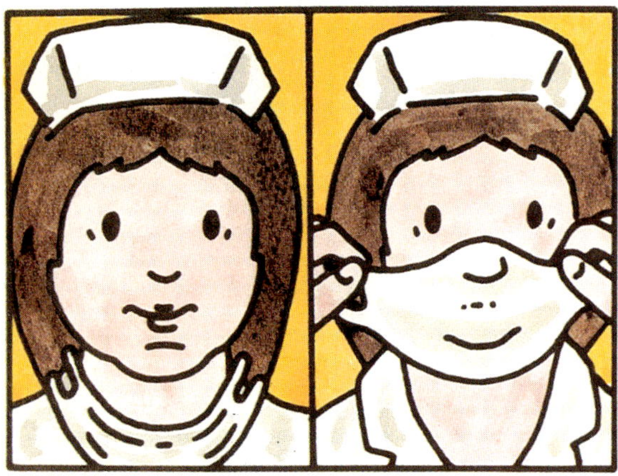

Then, when they tell you, you will see that hospitals aren't frightening at all. They are places where doctors and nurses help ill people get well.

One of the ways doctors help people get

well is by doing operations. That means they have to look inside a person's body to see what is wrong.
It's just like looking inside a car engine to see what is wrong.
But people don't have lids over their insides, the way cars have lids over their engines.
It would be useful if we did, wouldn't it? Because we haven't, the doctor has to make an opening so that she can look inside. It would hurt if she did that while you were awake, so she stops it hurting by sending you to sleep before you have an operation. She has a doctor to help her who gives you a special medicine called an anaesthetic to send you to sleep.

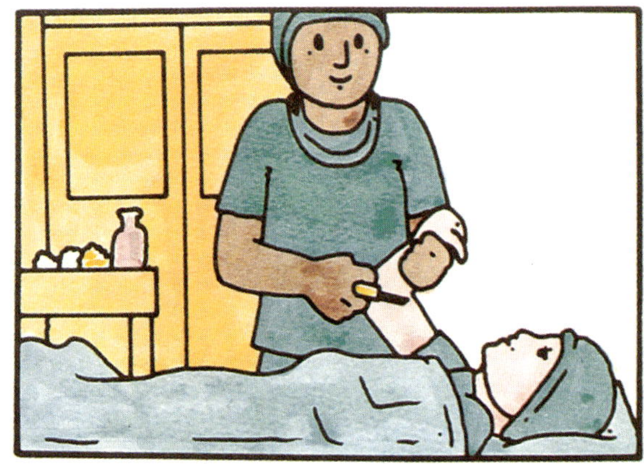

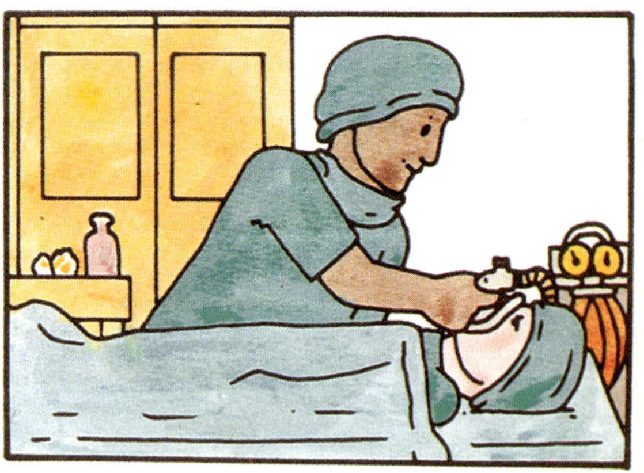

Can you remember what the word anaesthetic means? (If you aren't sure, look again at page 30.)
When you are asleep the doctor makes an

opening in you to take away what shouldn't
be there.
Like an infected appendix
(your appendix is a bit of your gut that in
some people gets so full of germs it makes
them ill).
Or infected tonsils
(tonsils are places in your throat where
germs are caught to stop them getting deep
inside you. If they get too full of germs they
can make a person feel ill).
Sometimes operations have to be done to
mend something that isn't working right.
Like eyes that squint –
or ears that need grommets –
or hearts that aren't pumping blood
properly –
or feet that are shaped the wrong way.
After the operation has been done, the
doctor sews up the opening she made, and
the person goes back to bed in the ward
with all the other ill people who are there
to get well.

After you have had an operation, you don't
feel very comfortable.
The place where the doctor made the
opening hurts.
You feel tired and sad.
But after a while, you begin to feel better.
Your family comes to visit you and brings
you toys and fruit.
Your friends send you cards.
You talk to the other children and play with
them.
Now being in hospital can be fun. There is a
lot to see and a lot to do.
You can play with toys –
and jigsaws –
and you can paint and draw and make
models and do all the things you enjoy
doing.
To stop you losing bits of your games under
the blankets, ask the nurse to fasten a big
towel round your middle and use it to
cover the bed. Then everything you're

playing with stays on top and can't slip
down inside.
If you have to stay in bed at home, while
you are getting better from a cold or a
cough or German measles or mumps or
chicken pox, your mother or father can do
the same for you.
It's a very good way to keep you
comfortable.
It is also a good way to stop itchy crumbs
getting into your bed.

Most of the people who go to hospitals because they are ill, and most of the people who have operations, get completely well. But not all of them do.

Some people have things wrong with them that can never be made well.

They can't walk —

they can't run about —

they can't think and talk and do things as easily as other people.

They may have to be in wheel chairs all the time.

Or they may need special braces on their legs to help them get about or covers on their heads to stop them banging them.

People like this are called disabled. They may have problems, but they can still be happy people.

If you meet people who are disabled, talk to them the same way you would talk to people who are not disabled.

They aren't funny or peculiar, just because they are disabled.

They're just a little bit different.

Most people who get ill get better.
Children like you get ill and get better.
Grown ups like your mother and father and
aunts and uncles get ill and get better.
Old people get ill and get better.

But one day it happens that an old person
gets ill and doesn't get better.
The old person's body is tired of being
clever and fighting off illness, and making
new skin and bone when accidents happen.
So the old person dies.

Sometimes people who aren't old die.
But that doesn't happen very often.
It is usually only quite old people who die.
It is sad when people die because the
people who loved them feel lonely.
They miss them a lot.
It isn't so sad for the person that has died,
though, because they don't know they are
dead.
They are just comfortable and quiet and
have no more illnesses.

Pills and Potions Injections and Inhalations

However much care you take to be sensible and not have accidents –
to eat the right food –
and to have immunisations –
sometimes you will get ill.
Everybody does.
Sometimes when you are ill you need medicines.
Medicines can be liquids –
or pills –
or ointments –
or injections.
Doctors know all about them and decide which one is best for you. When you are ill, the doctor writes down on a prescription form which medicine you need, and the person at the chemist's shop then reads the prescription and makes the medicines ready for you.
Some pills are easy to swallow.
Some aren't.
If yours isn't, the best way is either to ask to have it squashed between two spoons, like this and mixed up with grated apple or fresh orange juice, or hidden in some honey.

But after eating the honey and the pill, make sure you drink water, to wash the stickiness off your teeth!
Some liquid medicines taste nice.
Some don't.
If yours tastes nasty, making a fuss won't make it taste any better.
Refusing to swallow it won't make you well.
The best thing to do is to take a deep breath –
Hold your nose –
Swallow it fast –
And then shout very loudly, "That was *HORRIBLE*!"
And then drink some water or eat a raisin or a piece of apple to take the taste away.
Doing that helps to make it easy to take nasty medicine.

If you have to have injections and don't like them —
(No one likes them much)
ask the nurse or the doctor to help you make it easier.
Say you will shut your eyes —
and count very loudly up to ten.
Tell them to give the injection on the number they choose, while you try to guess which number it will be.

If you think hard, trying to guess, you'll find you won't notice the injection nearly so much when it happens.
After the injection has been done, ask the doctor or nurse to rub the place hard.
That helps to stop it hurting.

Do you know there are some people who have to have injections every single day?
Every single week?
Year after year after year?
For ever and ever?
They have an illness called diabetes. That means that their bodies aren't good at digesting sugar properly.
They need special medicine called insulin.
Insulin has to be given in injections.
Every day of every week of every year for ever and ever.
Lots of very young children have injections like that and they don't mind because they know the injections make them well.
Because doctors give people medicines and injections only when they need them.

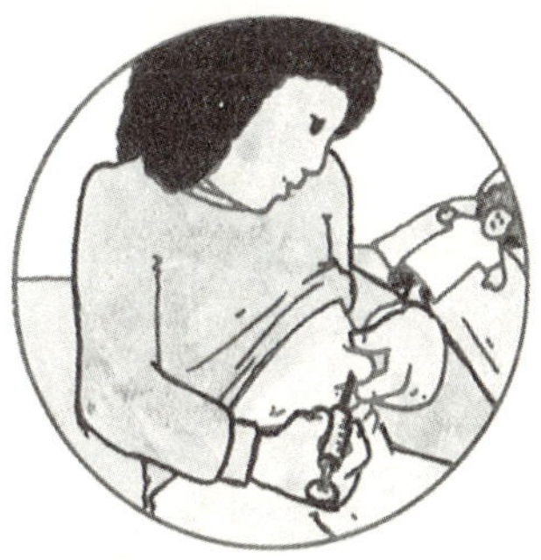

Taking Care

Has hearing about all the different ways there are of being ill made you sad?
Has it made you think that you are going to be ill a lot?
Don't think that.
People can take care of themselves so that they don't get ill too much.

You can make sure you don't have silly accidents.
You can make sure you always use the Green Cross Code when you go out in the streets.
You can make sure you use the swings and the rocking horses and the roundabouts properly in the park.
You can make sure you learn to swim so that you can play safely on the beach and at the pool.
You can make sure you learn the right way to hold a knife and scissors and sharp tools so that you don't get cuts.
You can make sure you don't play with matches or electrical things, so that you don't get burns.

You can learn to take care and not have silly accidents and still have fun.
You can climb trees.
And frames in the park.
You can swim and dive,
Jump and run.
And have all sorts of adventures.
It's just doing silly things that could hurt you that can make you ill.
Like climbing into places where you aren't supposed to go.

And showing off.

There are other ways of taking care of
yourself and not getting ill.
Eating the right food is a way of taking care.
Sweets and ice-creams and fizzy drinks and
sugary cakes may seem good but they
aren't.
First of all, they can stick on your teeth.
Germs like sugary things, and when they
get into your mouth from the air, they jump

on the sugar and gobble it up.
When germs gobble sugar they make acid
with it.
The acid can hurt your teeth, and make
them black, and ugly, and very, very sore.
That is why it is important to brush your
teeth, and wash away the sugar and the
germs.

But it's best of all not to eat the sugar.
Instead, eat apples and carrots and cabbage
stalk and celery.
They taste sweet and chewy, but they don't
make teeth sticky. Sweets and ice-creams
and fizzy drinks and sugary things aren't
only bad for teeth.
They are bad for other bits of your body as
well.

They turn into fat, but not into muscle, which is what your body needs more than fat.
To make muscles you need to eat good white fish and chicken and fresh vegetables and peas and beans and crunchy brown bread and cheese and eggs.
You don't want too much of them.
Just enough!
Then you'll have a strong healthy body that can jump and play and laugh and sing and make new skin when you have accidents and fight off germs and make antibodies.

Eating the right food isn't the only way of taking care of yourself.
Your body can be helped to make antibodies without having an illness first.
Can you remember what happens when you get German measles and mumps and chicken pox?
You get spots and lumps and coughs and sneezes and feel miserable.
But while you feel like this, your body is making antibodies so that you don't get the German measles and mumps and chicken pox ever again.

There are other illnesses children used to get.
Whooping cough, diphtheria and tuberculosis, polio and tetanus.
They were very horrible illnesses.
Some children got so ill that they never got better.
But now these illnesses don't happen the way they used to, because children can be given special medicines to stop them.
This is called immunisation.
Babies are given injections to help their bodies make antibodies for these illnesses.
Ask your family which immunisations you had when you were a baby.
Isn't it good to know such good care has been taken of you?

So now you know all about what happens when people are ill, and how they get better.
You know how clever your body is.
Isn't it good to have such a clever body?